SING WITH ME!

Color with me says Llama Louise
I draw pictures that aim to please...
Try to color between the lines
And make something to call mine
You can make it super pretty
Even if it's itty bitty!
Your beautiful creation can be hung on the wall,
Color it with your family and friends and have a ball!

Scan the QR code to
download my song!

Copyright © 2025 by [Renee' Marie Borowy]

All rights reserved.

The story, all names, characters, and incidents portrayed in this production are fictitious. No identification with actual persons (living or deceased), places, buildings, and products is intended or should be inferred.

Illustrated by Jumbo Blessing

Renee' Marie Borowy

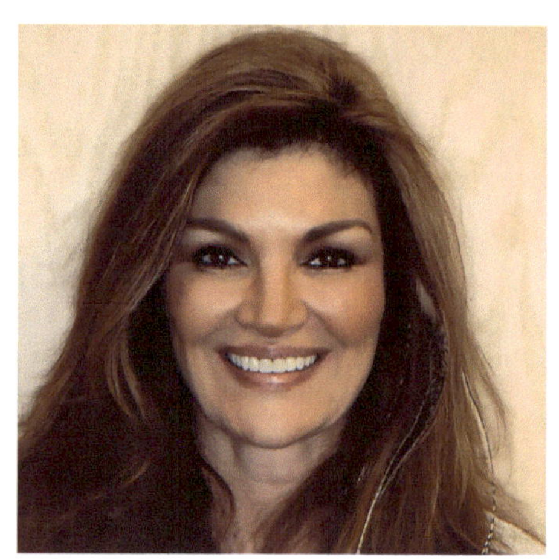

About the author

Renee' Marie Borowy is an avid animal lover. Recently retired from the beauty industry after 40 years, she has transitioned her creative skills into a career in writing. "I believe children's books are a wonderful way to help young minds understand complex issues in a way that resonates with them. Books provide a positive and meaningful way to share optimism and valuable life lessons." I look forward to creating several sequels and songs that complement each book.

LLAMA LOUISE SAYS:
COLOR WITH ME!!!

Color me as I sniff the flowers while a buzzing bee says hello!

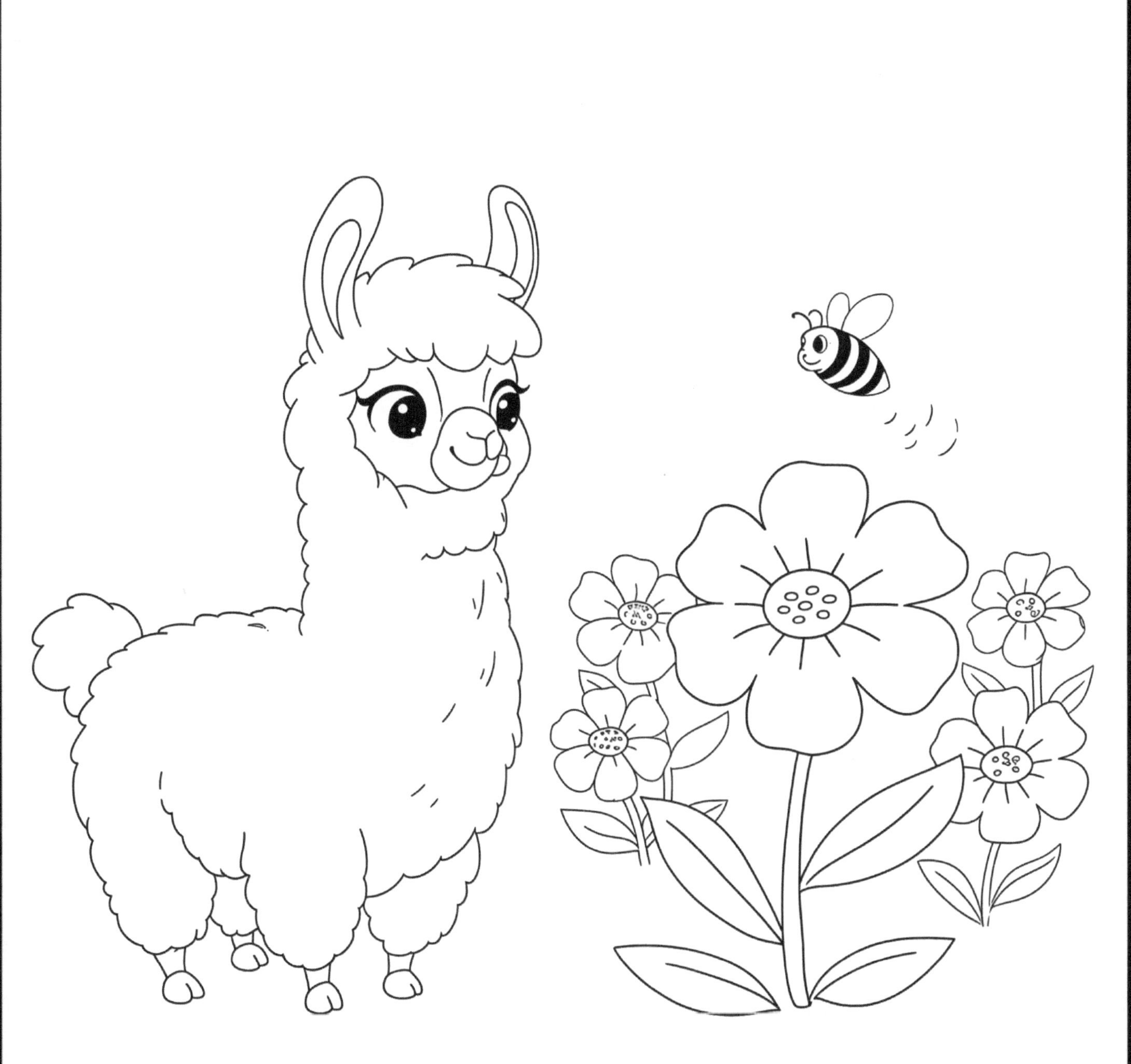

I'm standing proud! What color will you choose for my fur?

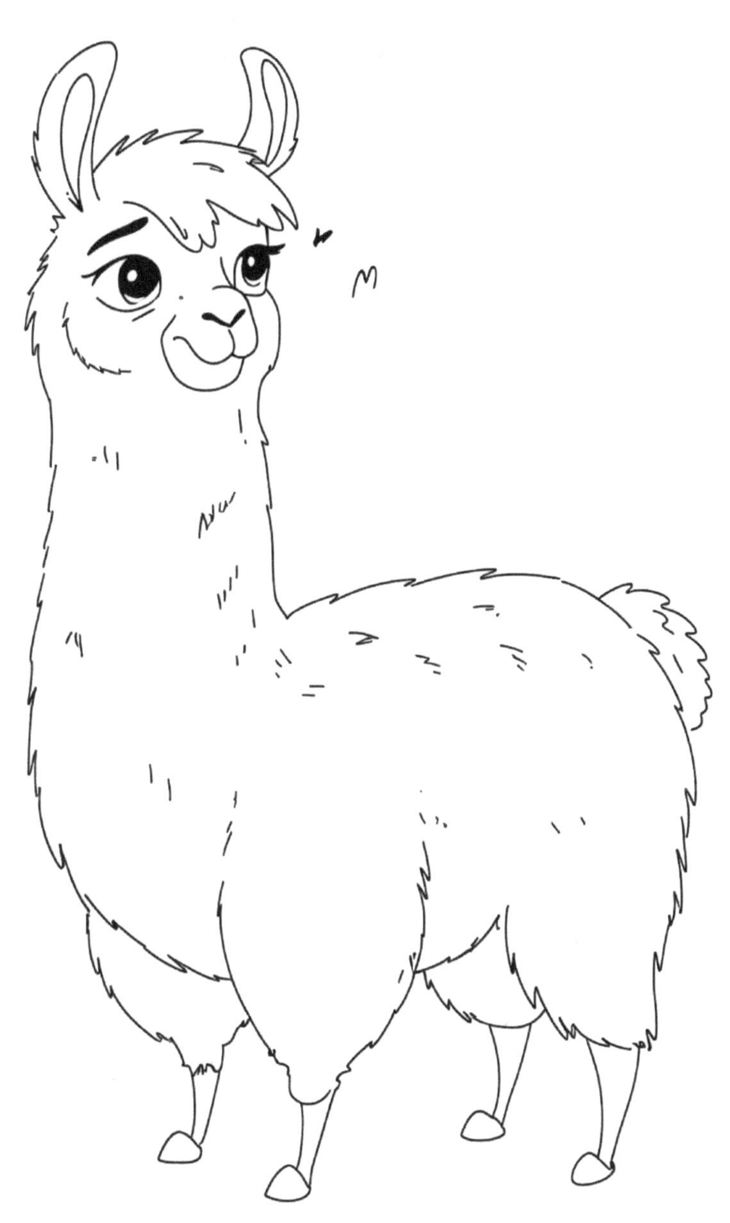

Color me smelling this flower... can you make it look sweet?

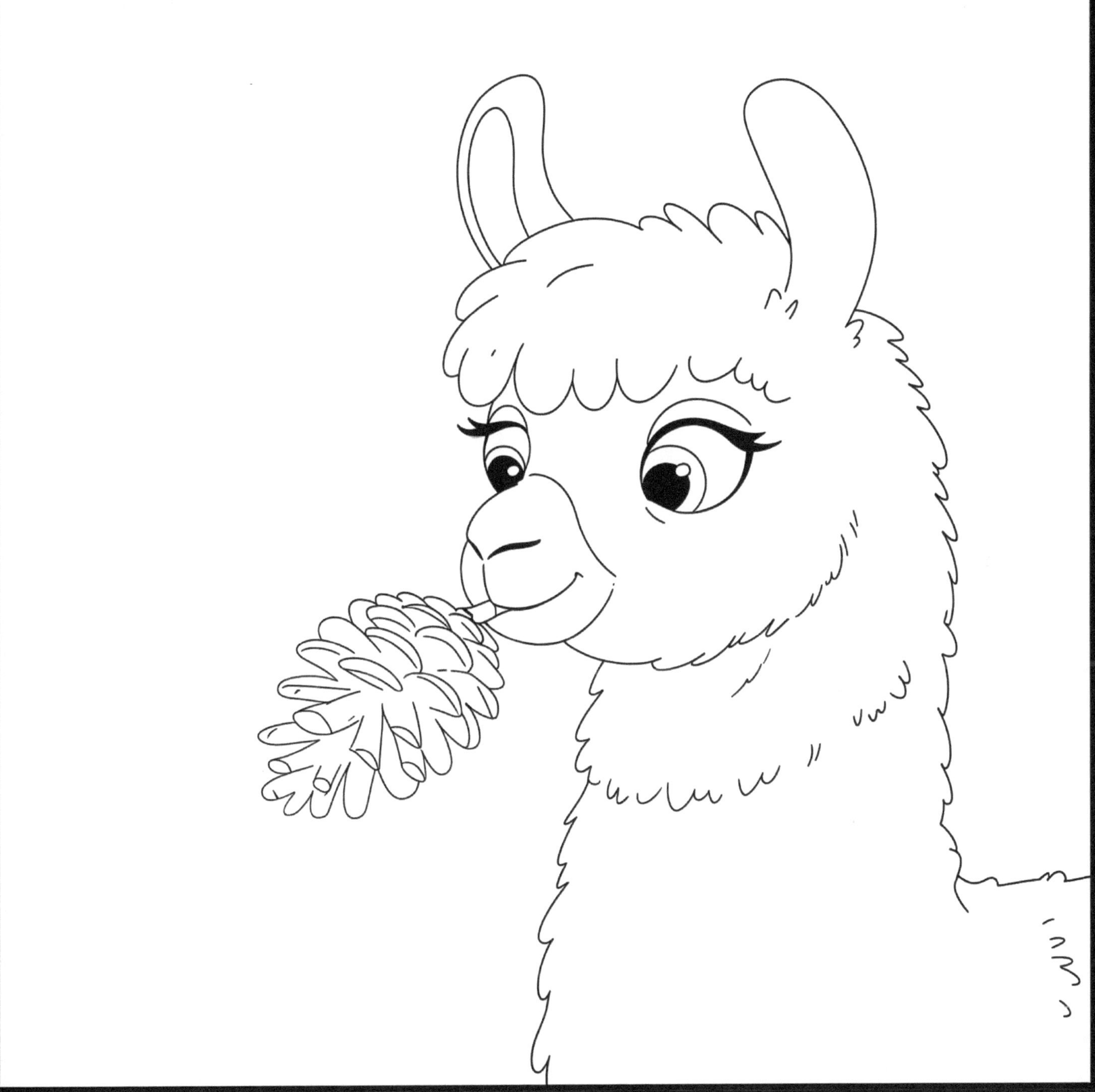

Can you color me and the apple near my feet and match it to your favorite fruit?

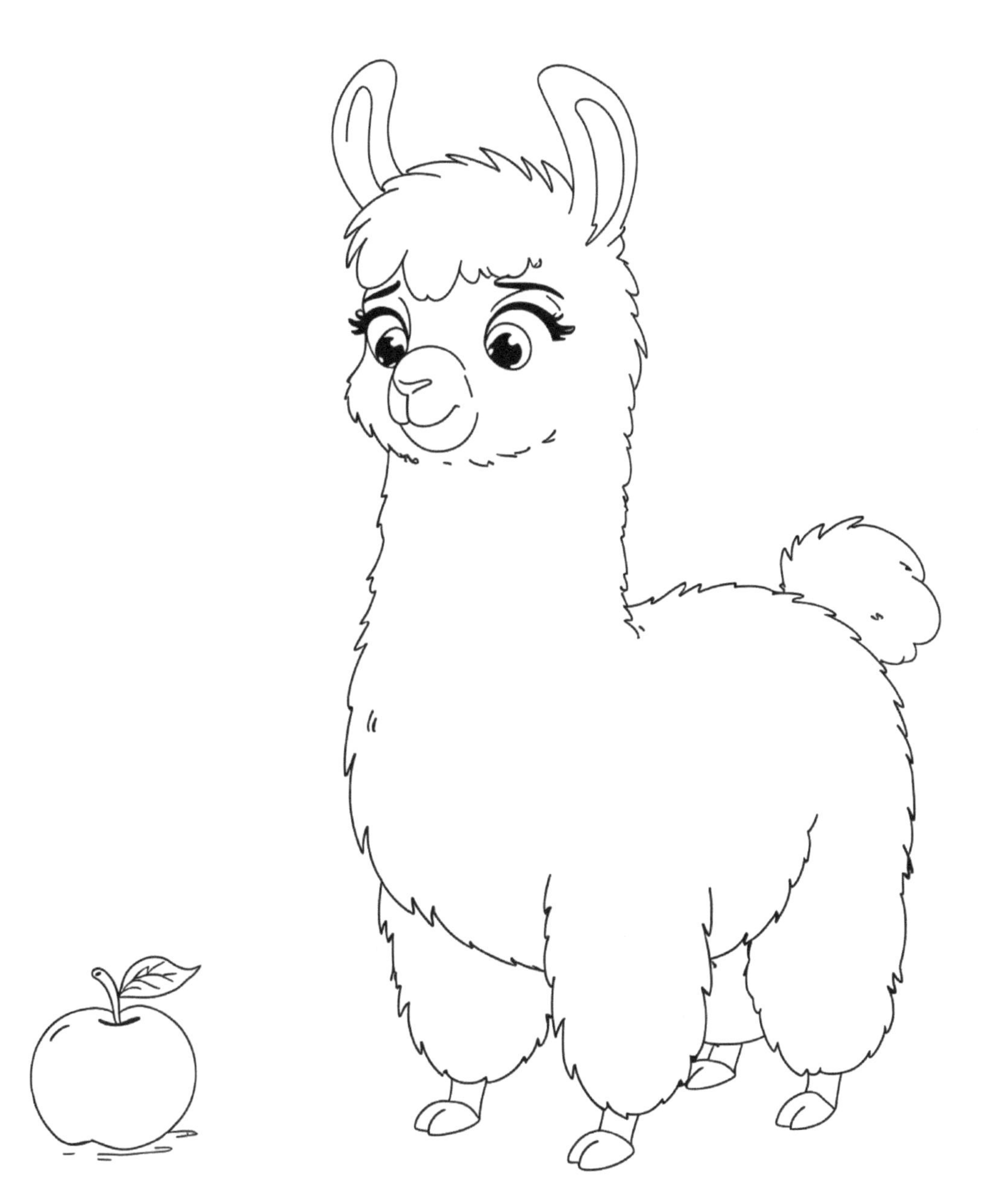

Look up! Color me and the little bird flying in the sky!

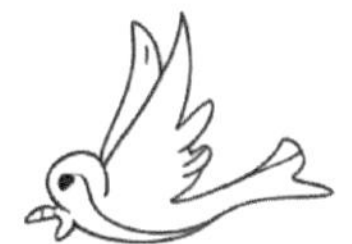
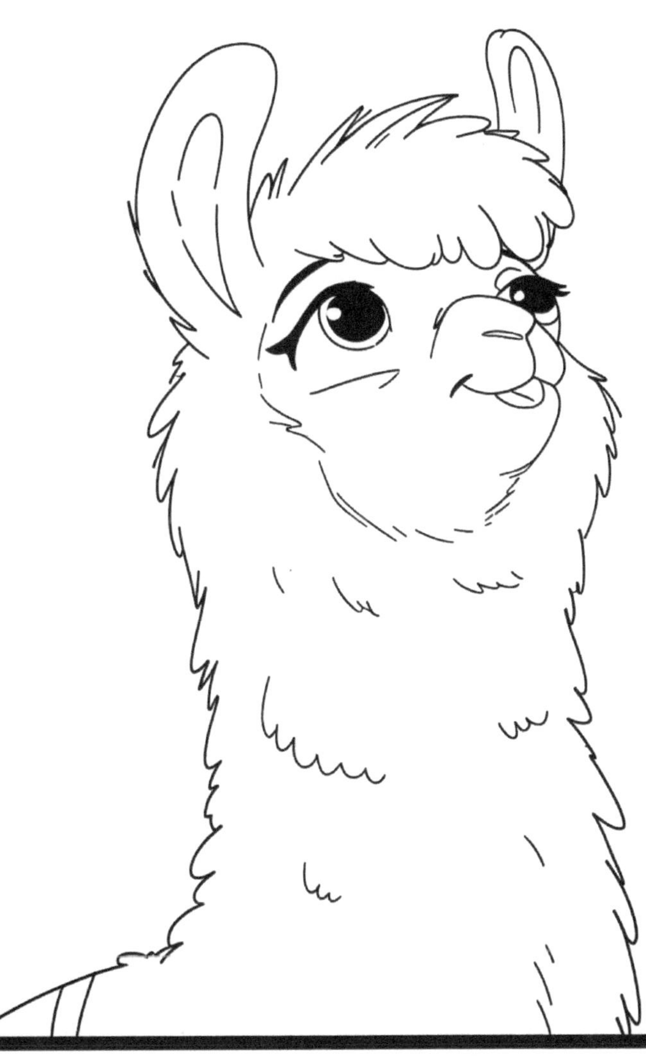

Let's play! Color me and my beach ball with your brightest shades!

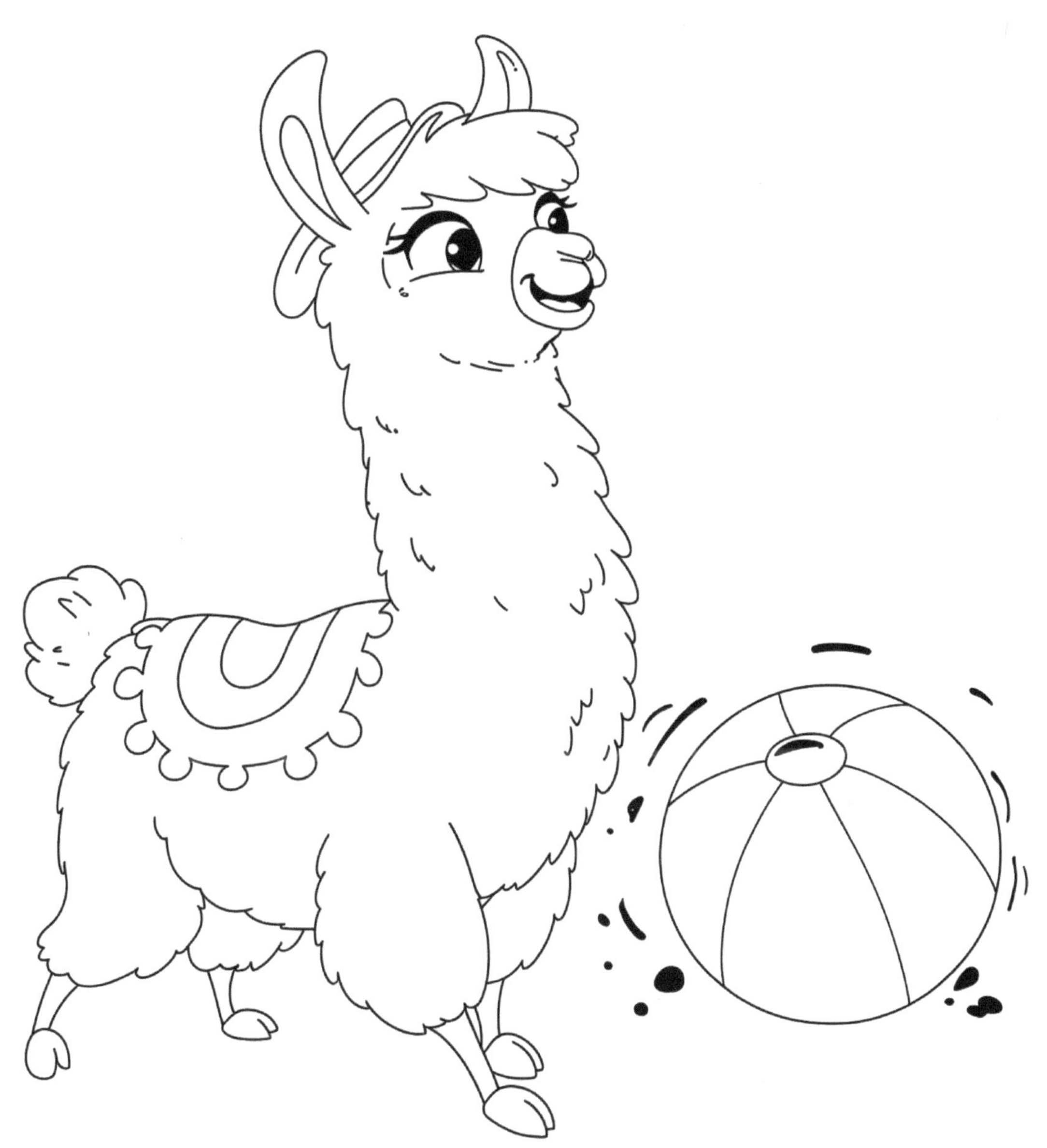

I'm flying a kite—what colors should the kite be?

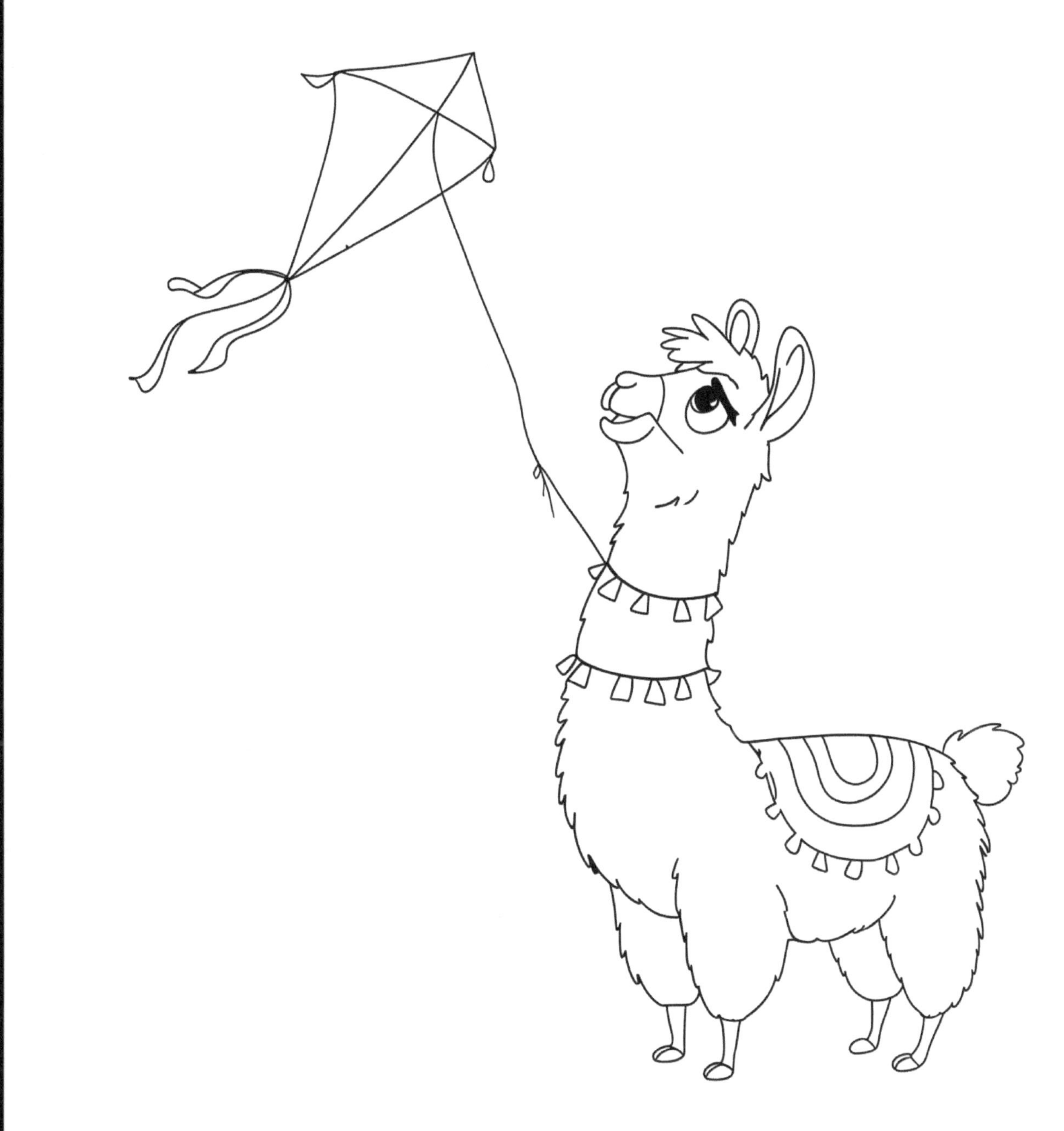

Color me walking with a leafy snack... yum!

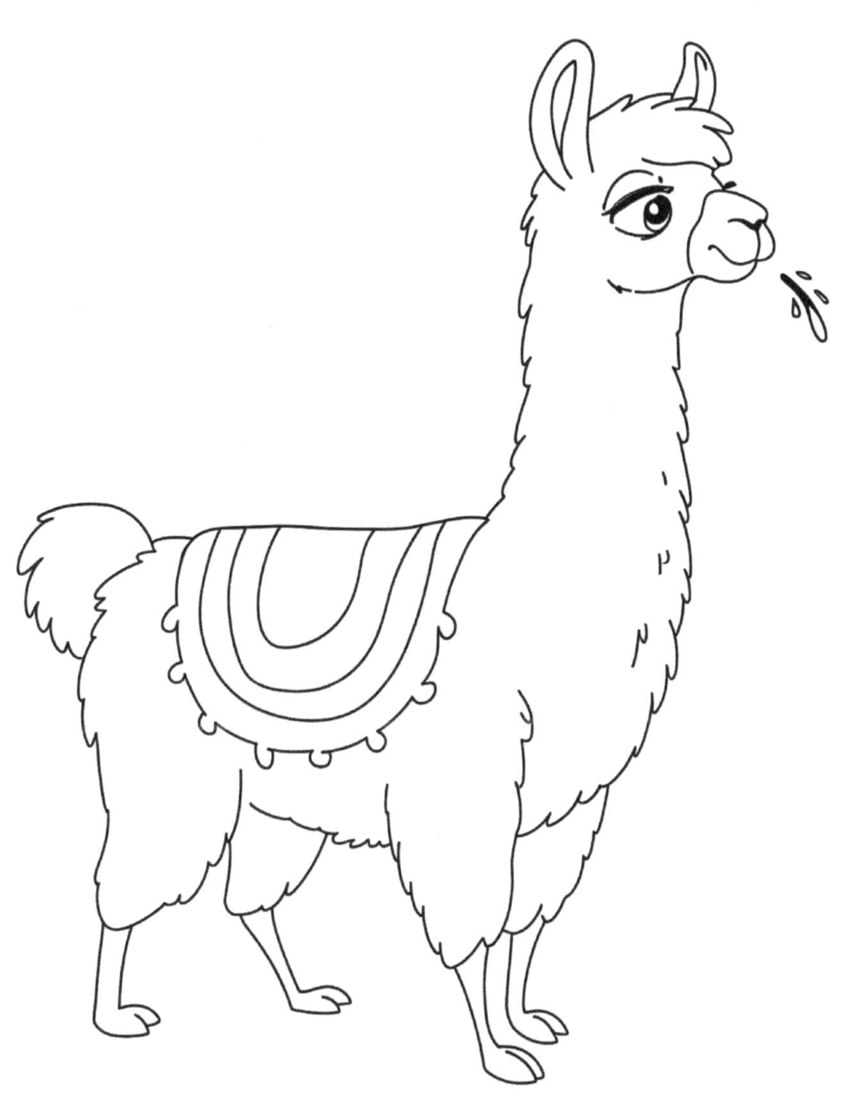

I'm feeling silly today; color my tongue and make me laugh!

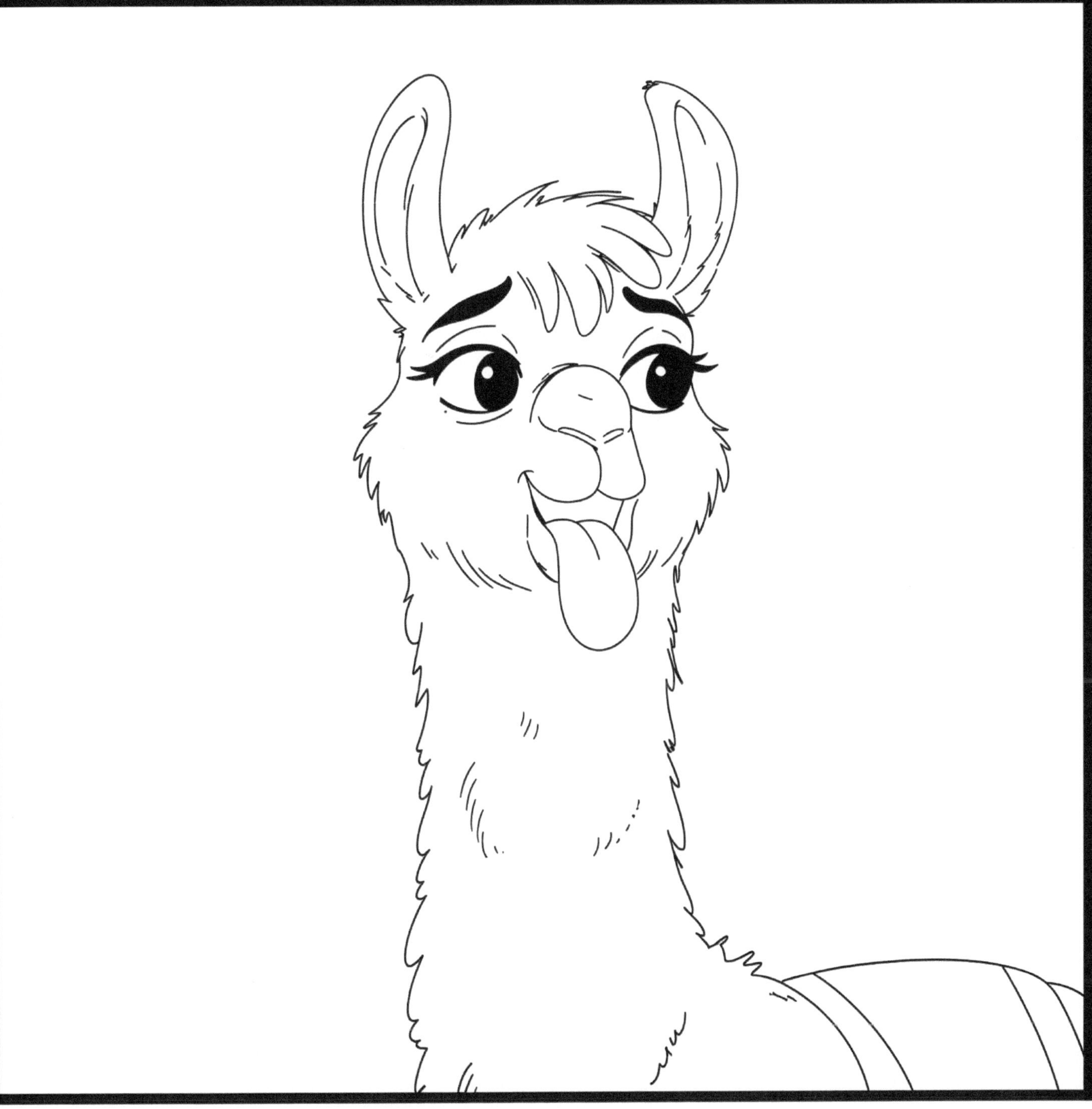

Shhh... I'm sniffing flowers. Can you color each petal a different color?

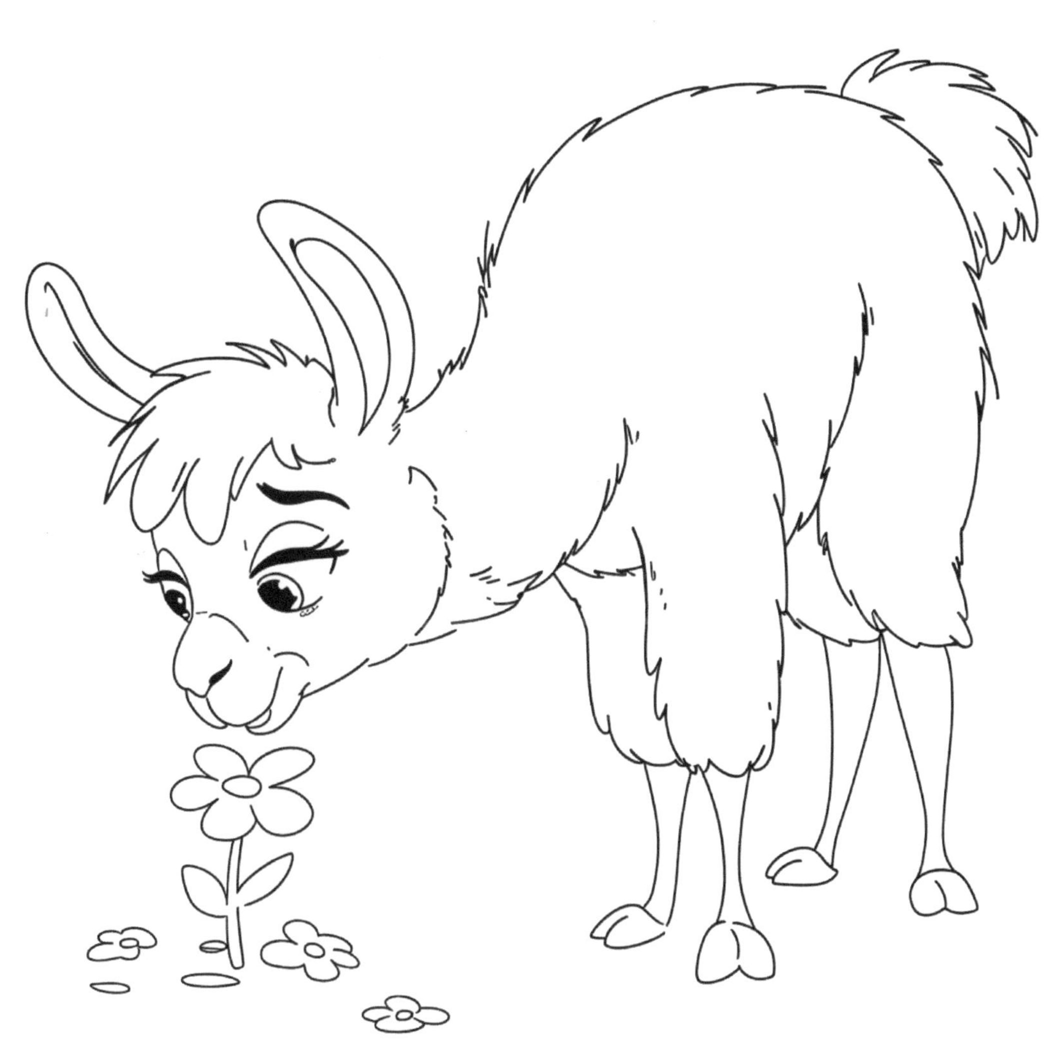

Color me hiding in the meadow while butterflies flutter by; can you count them all?

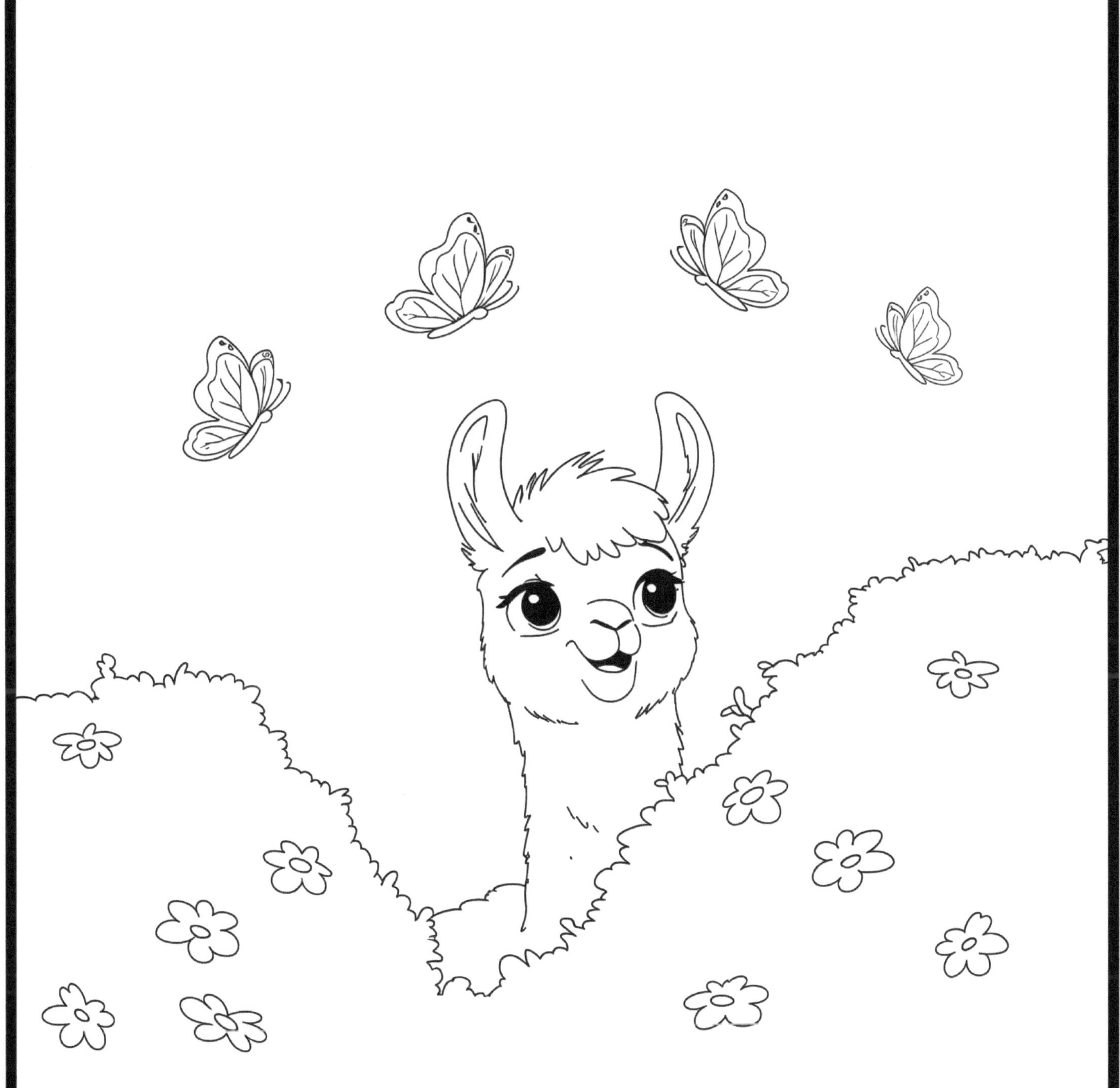

Color me sniffing these magical mushrooms; what colors will you choose for them?

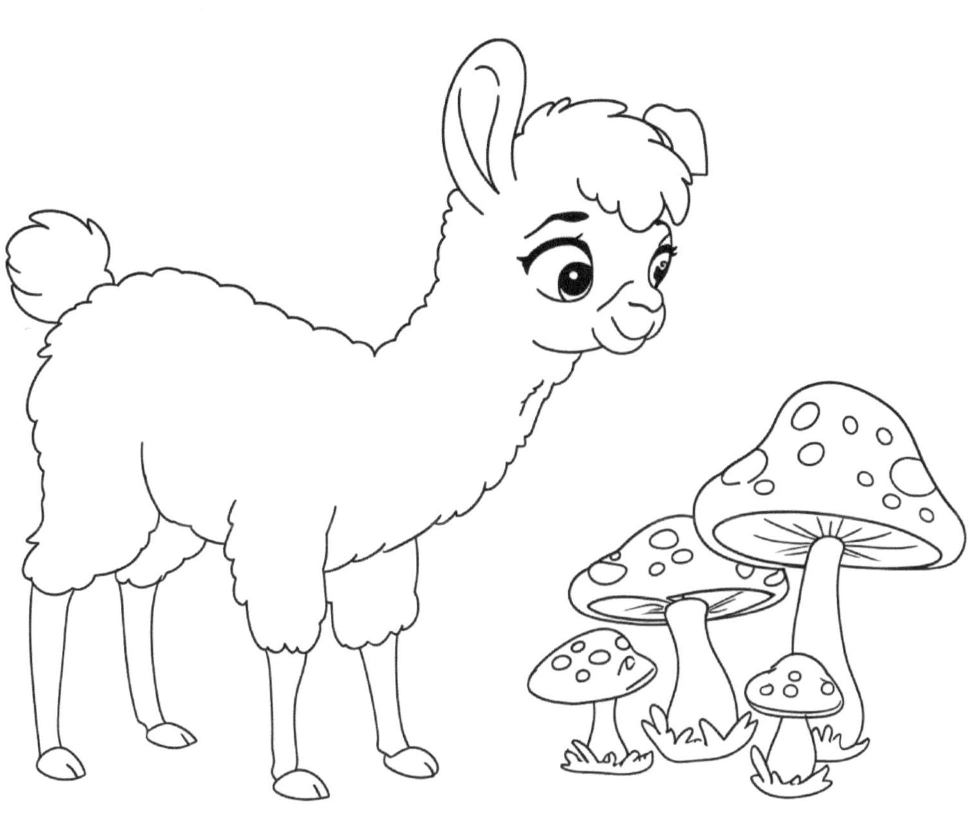

The wind is blowing
through my fur—color me
before I float away!

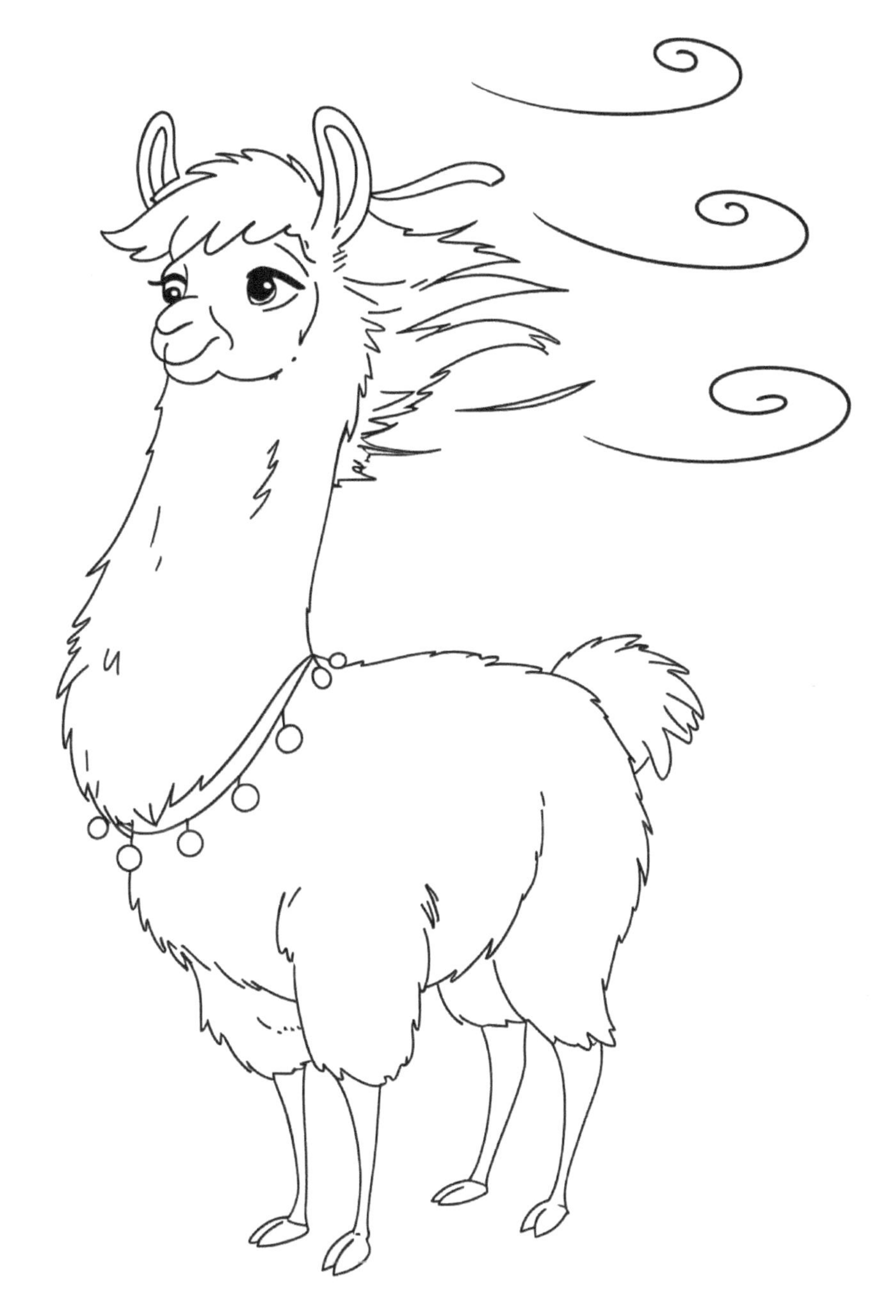

Color me enjoying a sunny picnic in my fancy little hat!

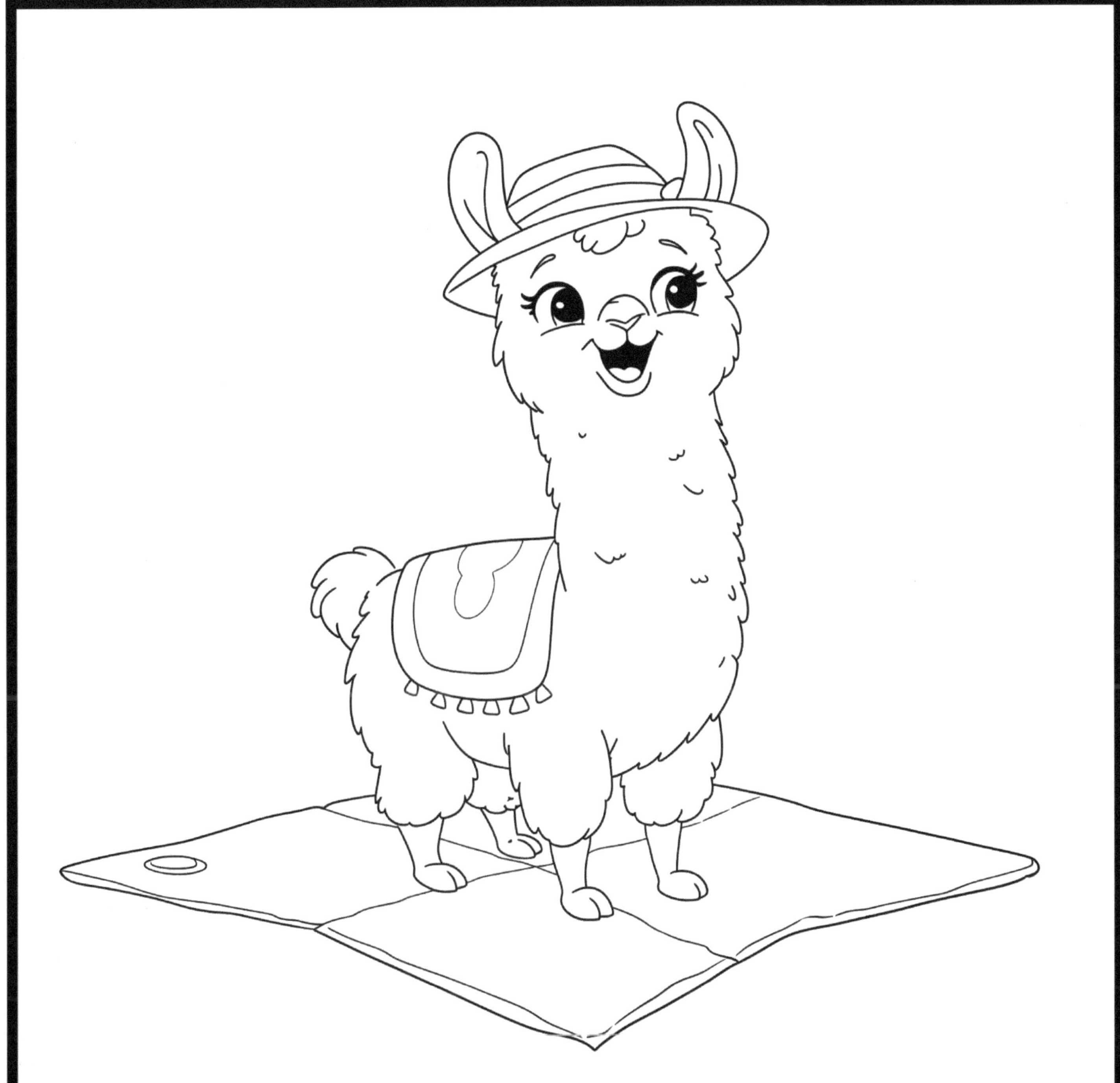

Splash! I'm jumping through puddles—color the water with your favorite blues!

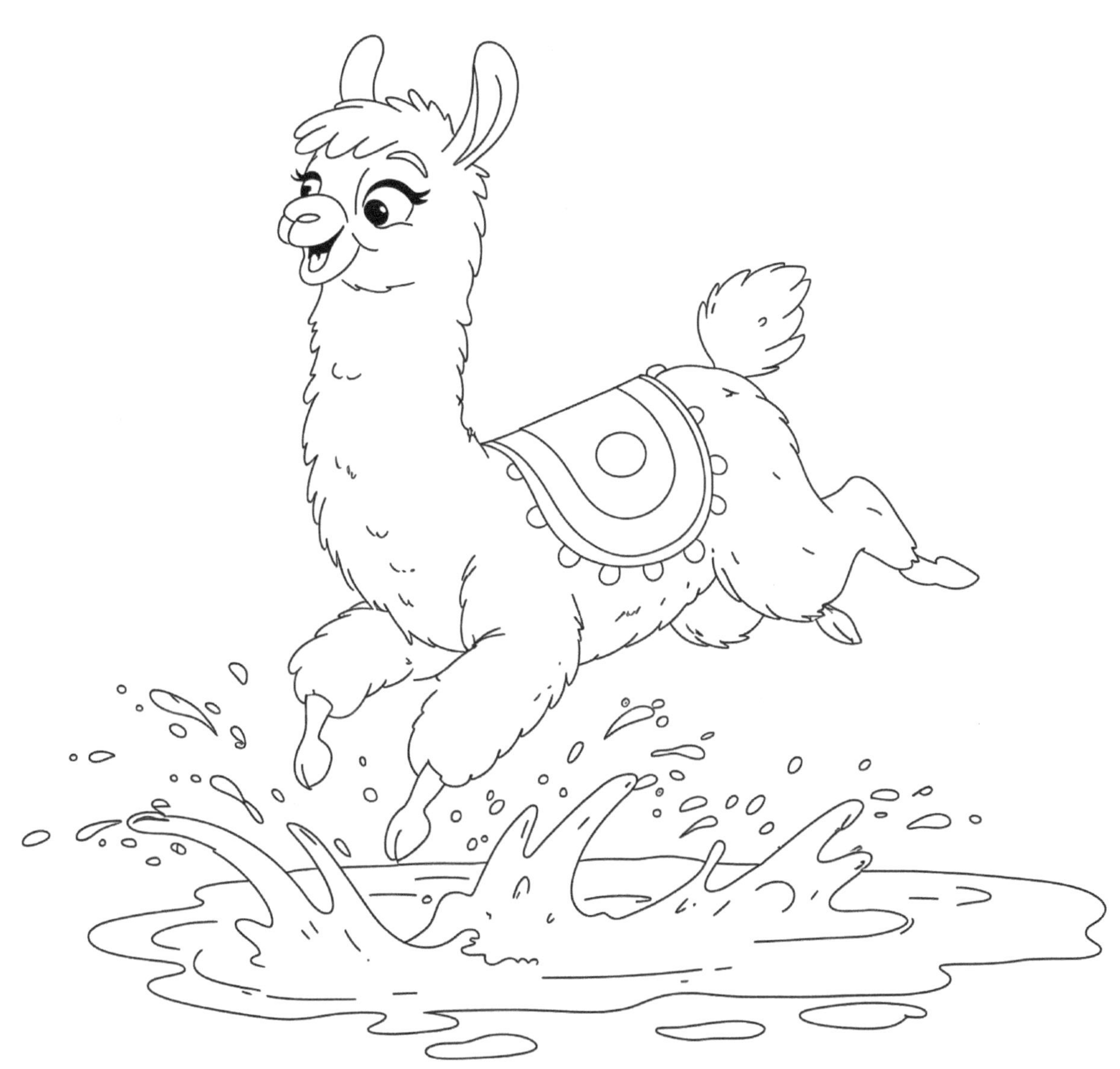

The man was astonished
by my beauty! What color
is his hat today?

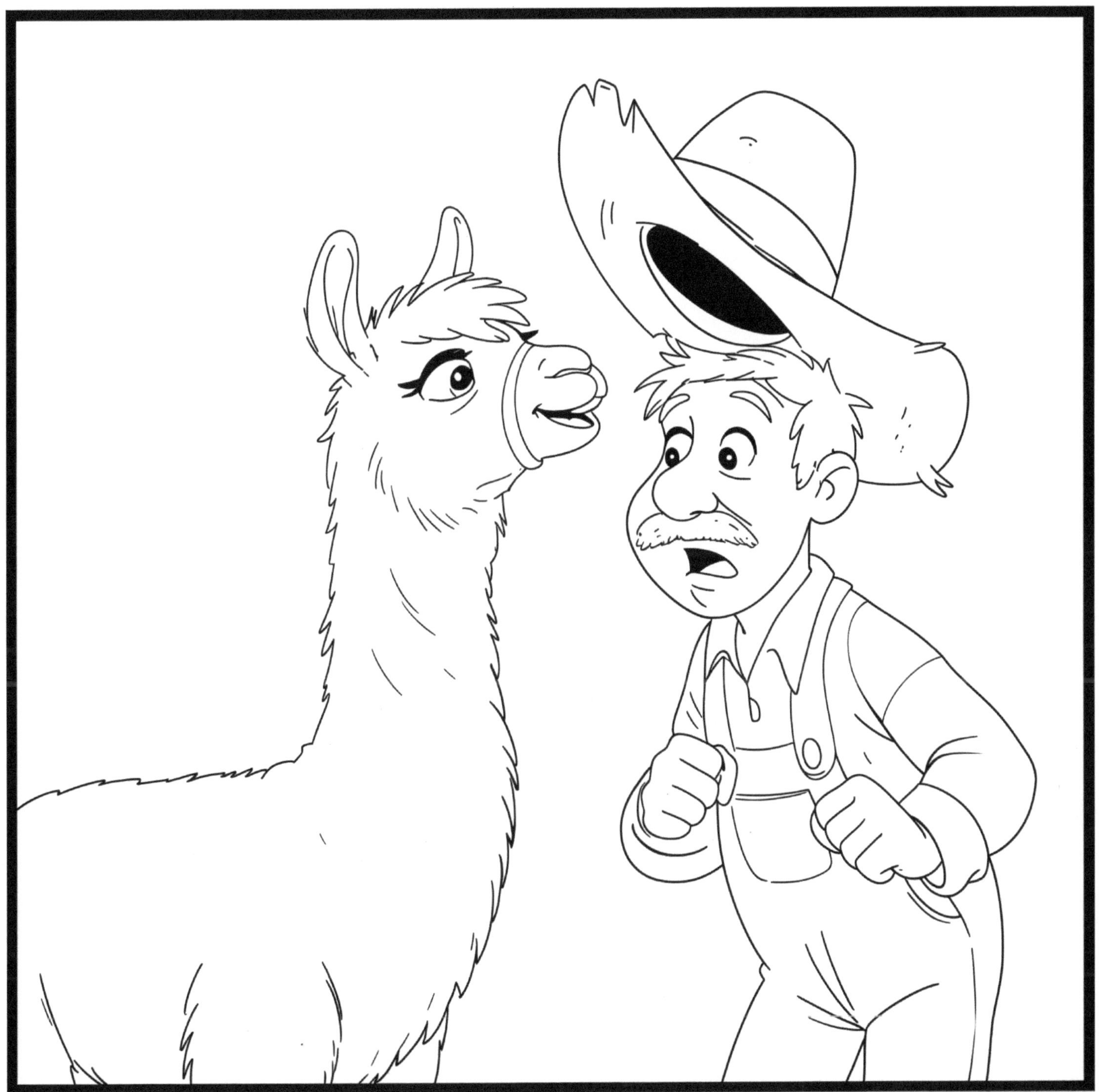

Guess who's here? It's my llama friend! Color us both with matching patterns!

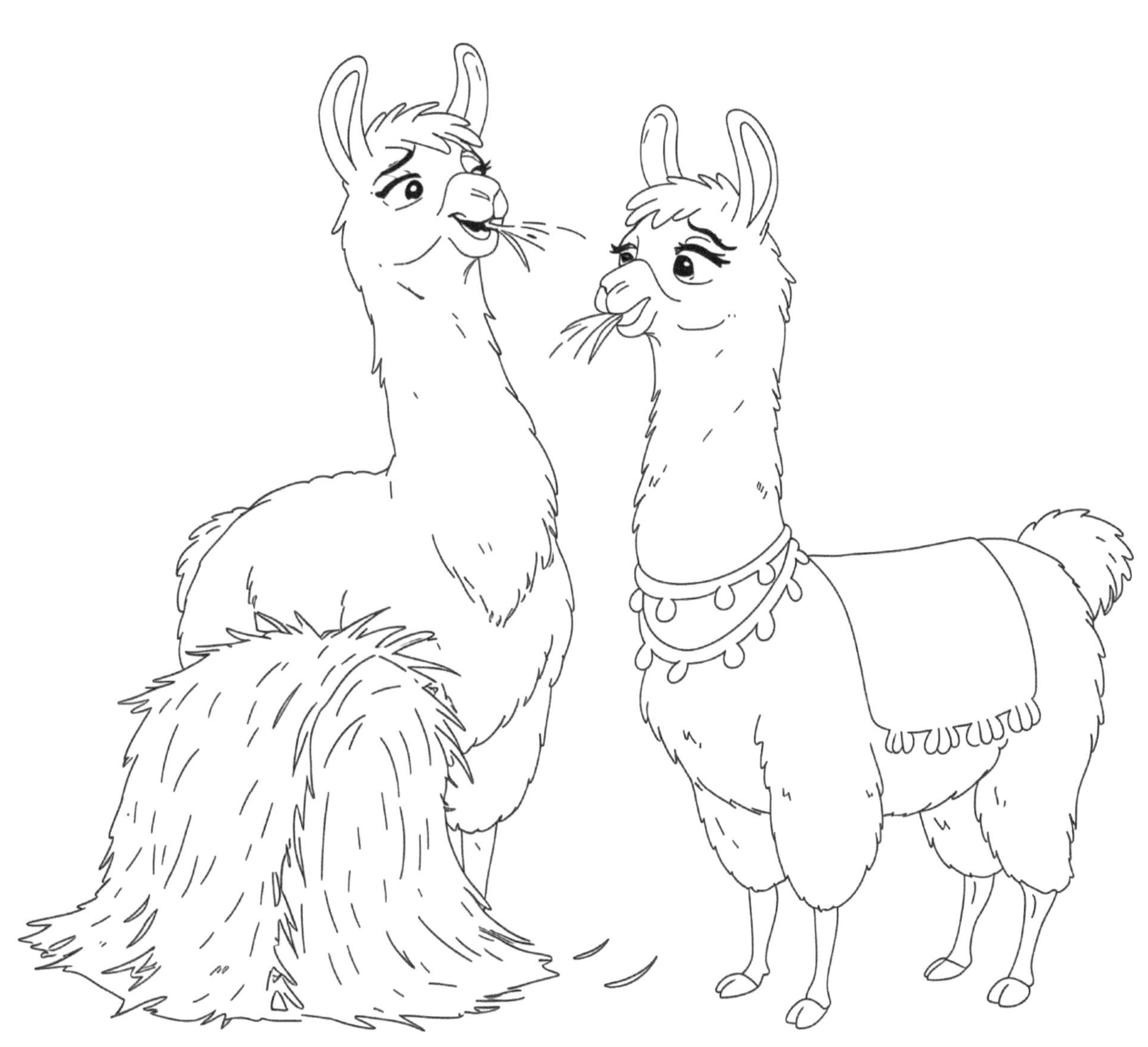

Farmer bob is brushing my fur; color us both and add sunshine if you like!

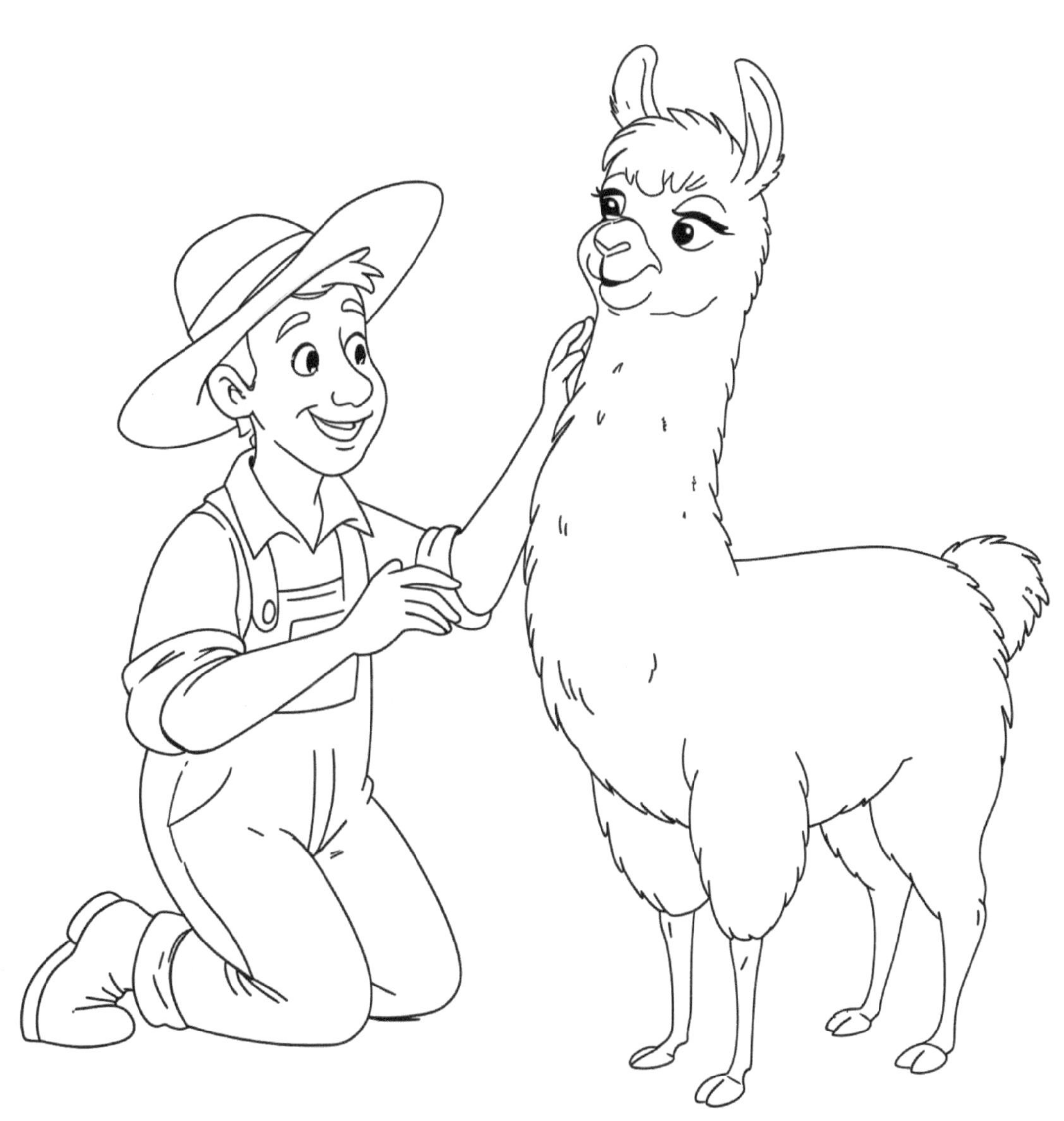

Color me and my piggy friend as we share a big pie; what flavor do you think it is?

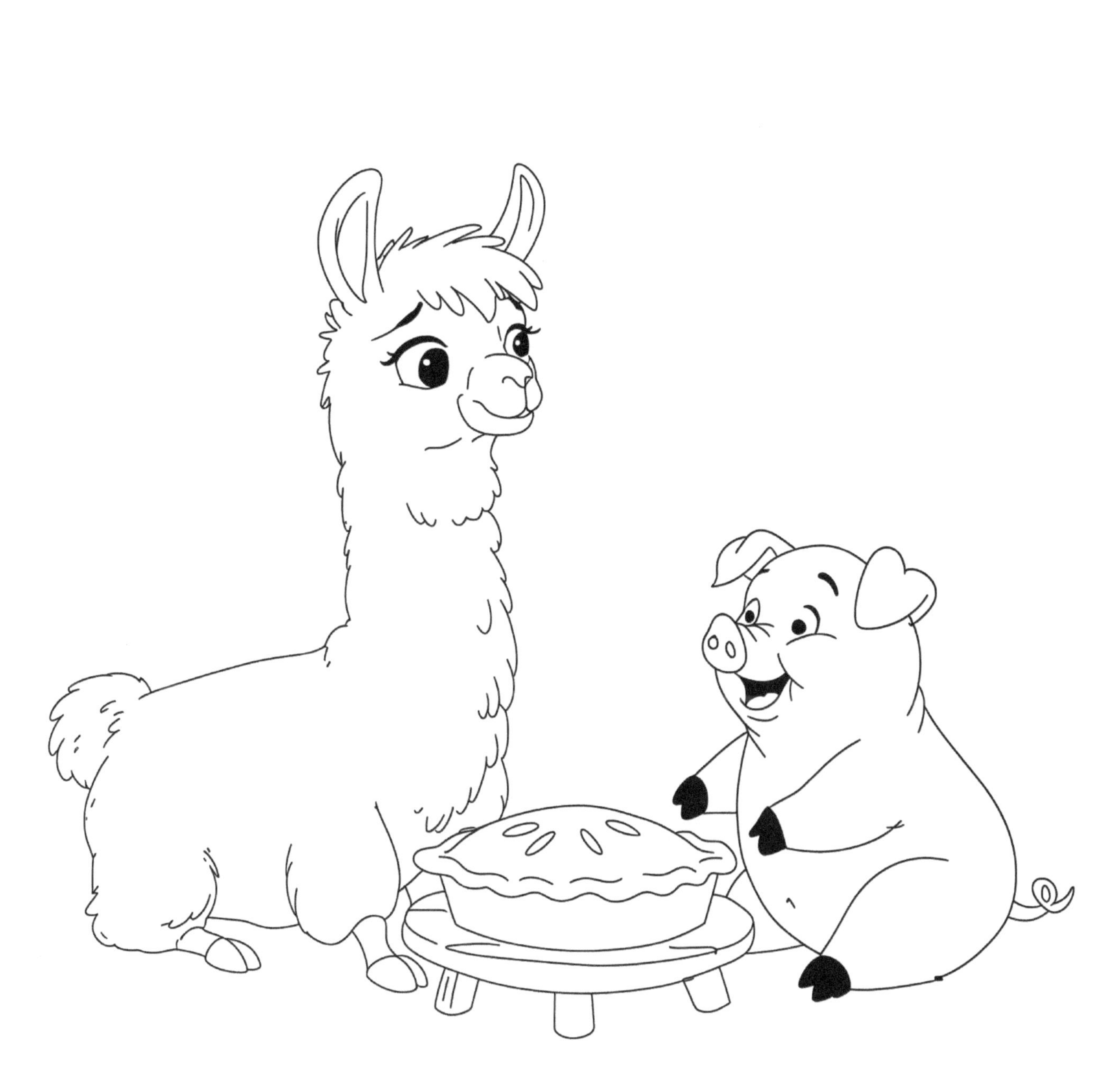

I'm taking a break in the sun; color me resting in the grass with cozy colors!

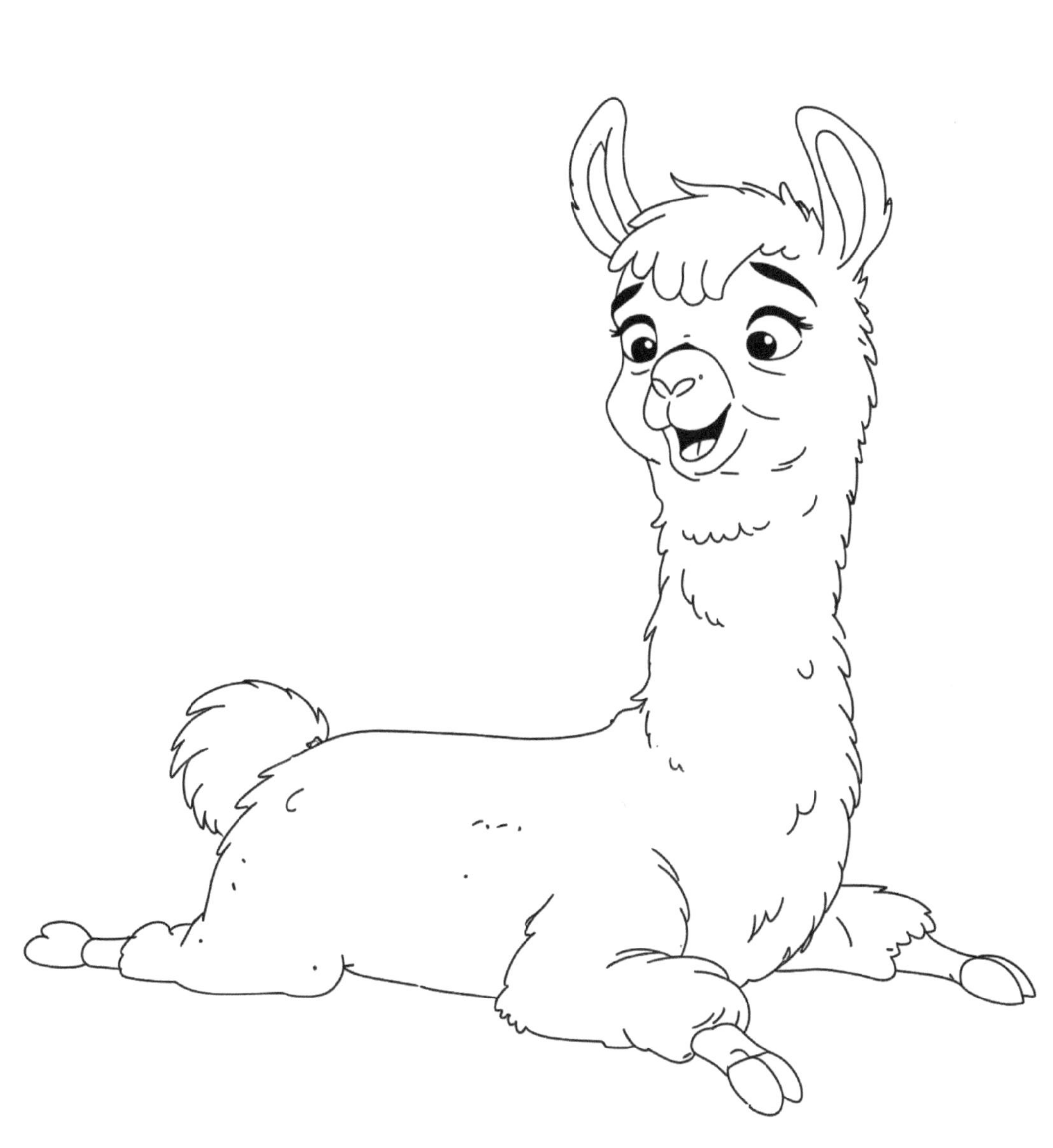

Color me standing near a boot and a bucket on the farm.

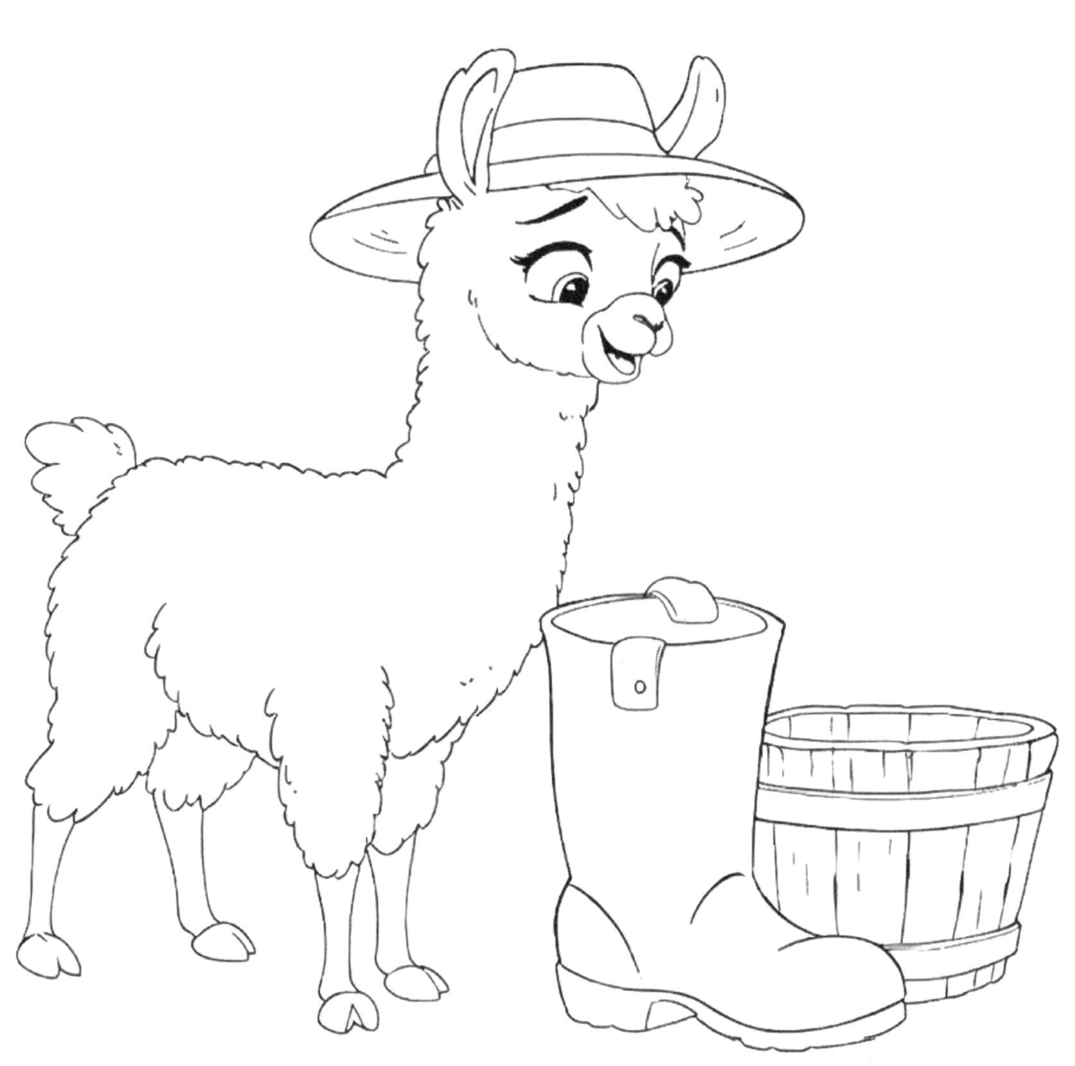

I found a cozy spot to rest with a cool drink beside me.

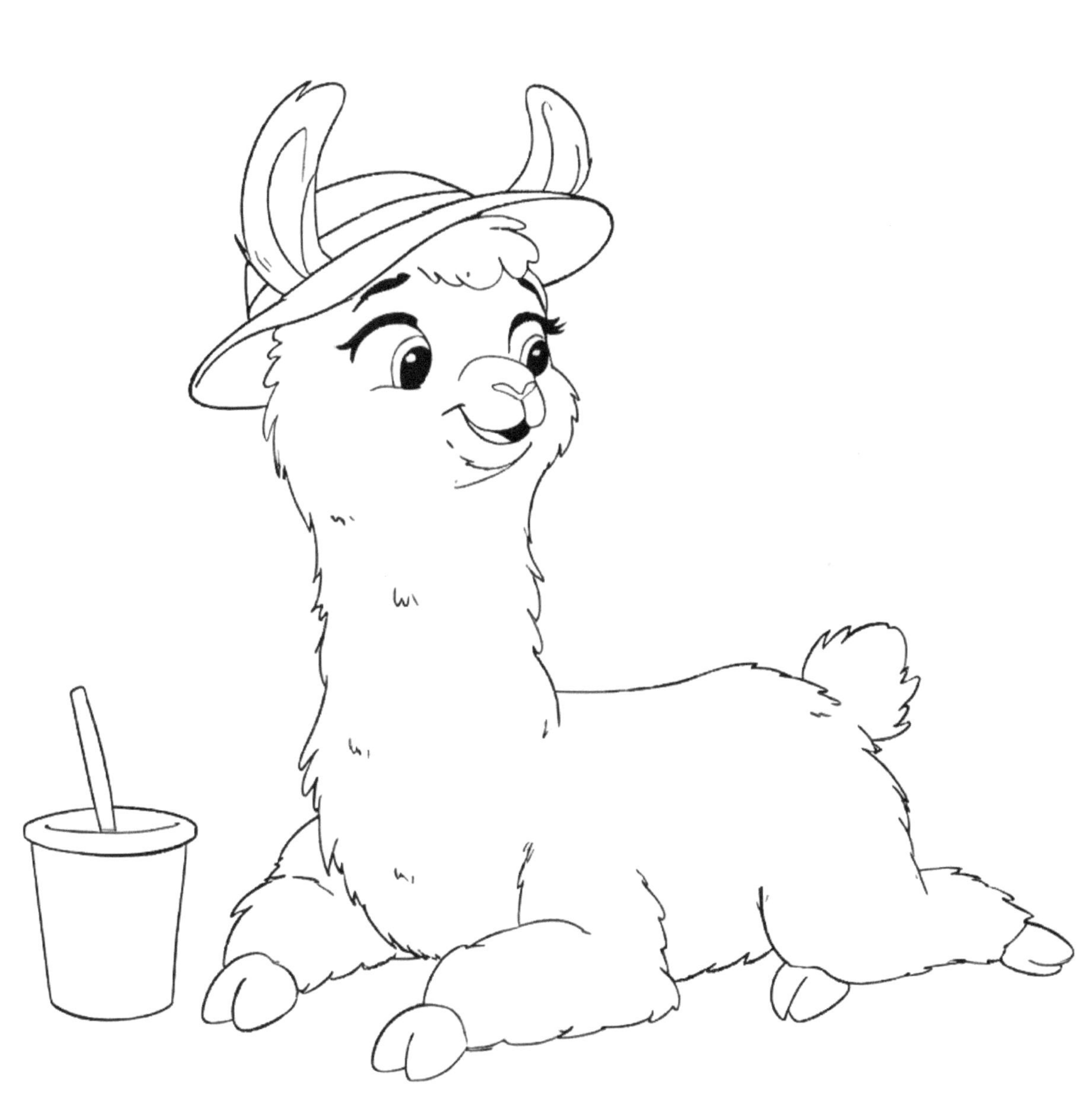

A tiny chick just hatched from its egg, ready to be colored.

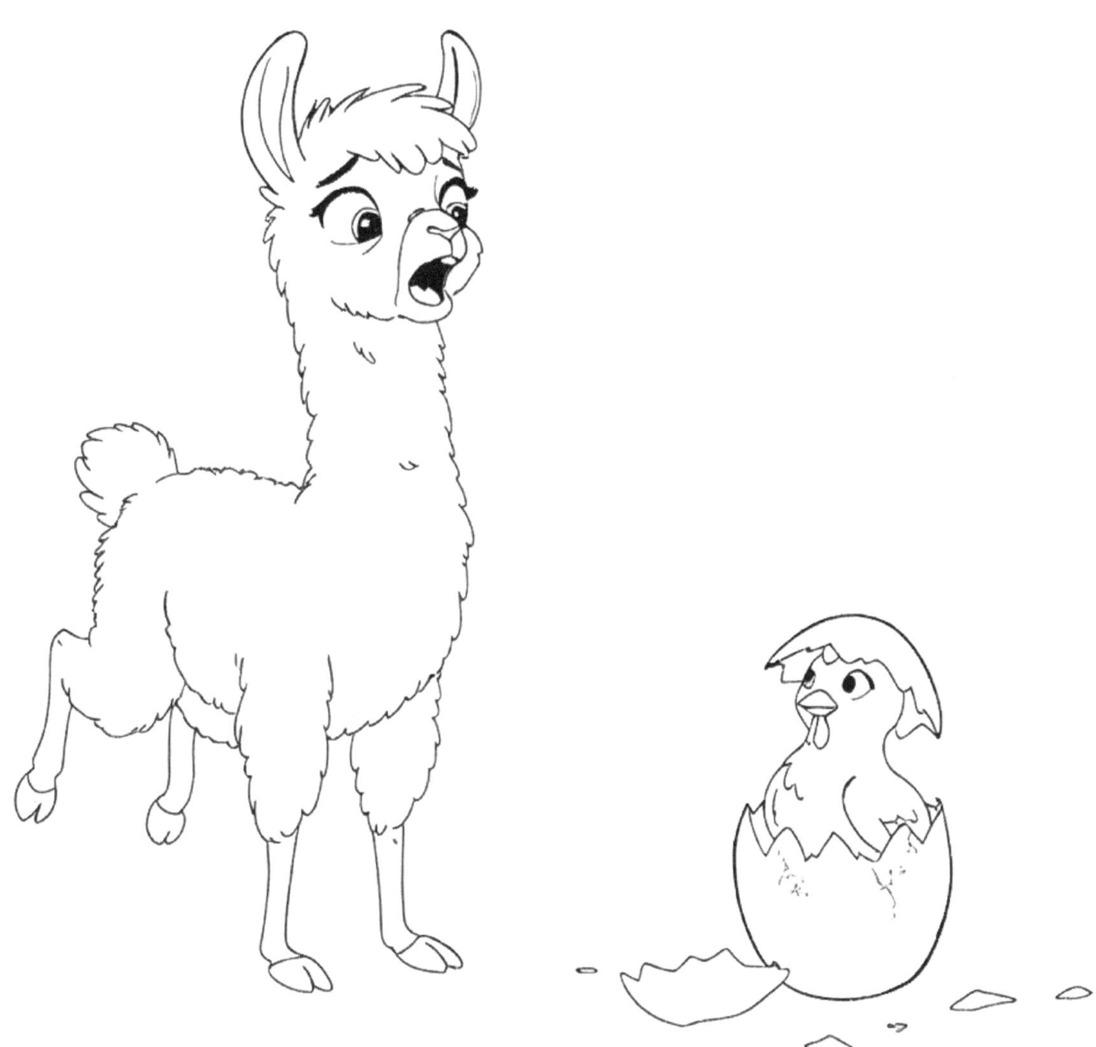

I spotted a round ball near my feet, what color will you give it?

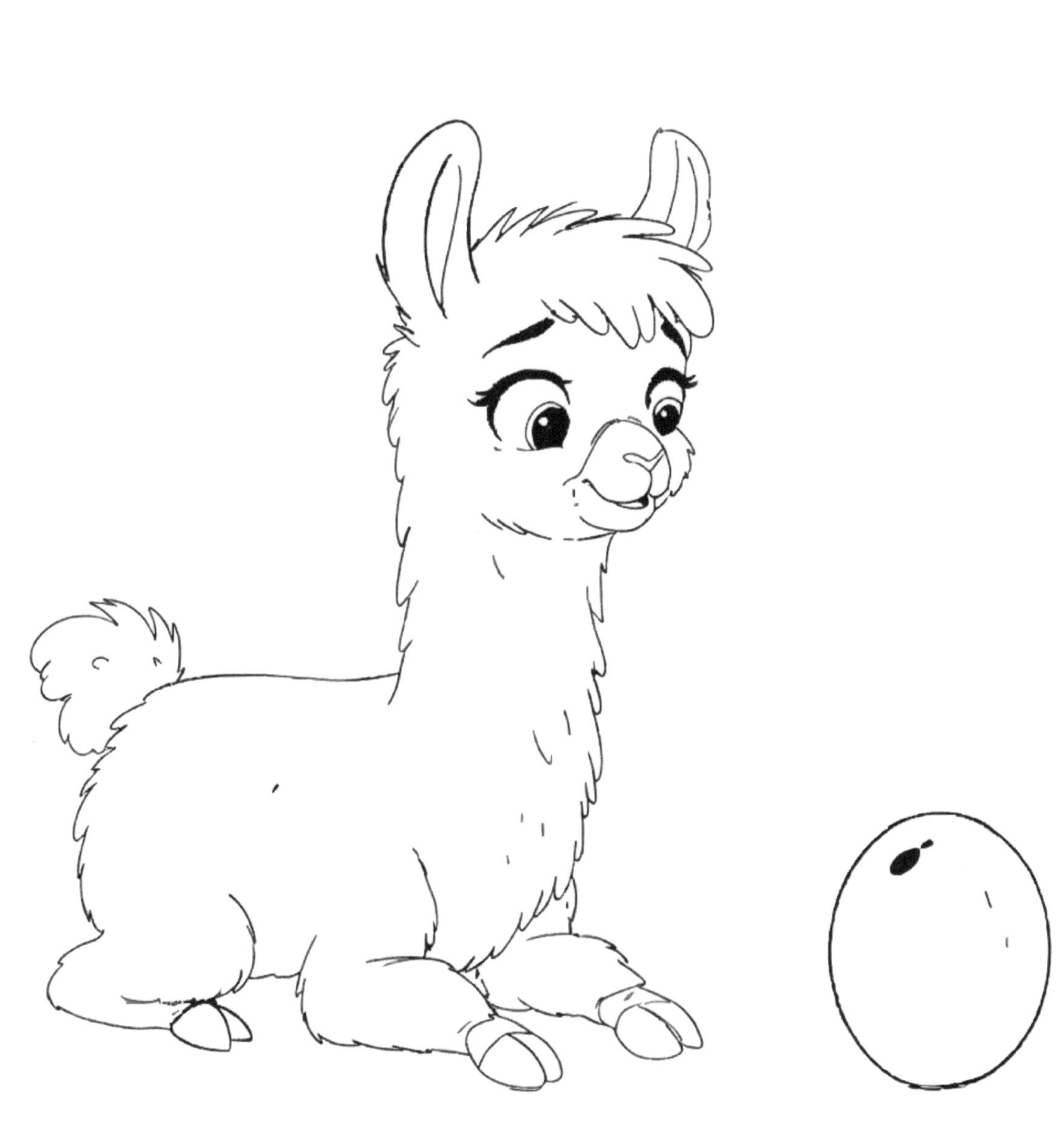

Snack time is here, color the cup and my fluffy fur too!

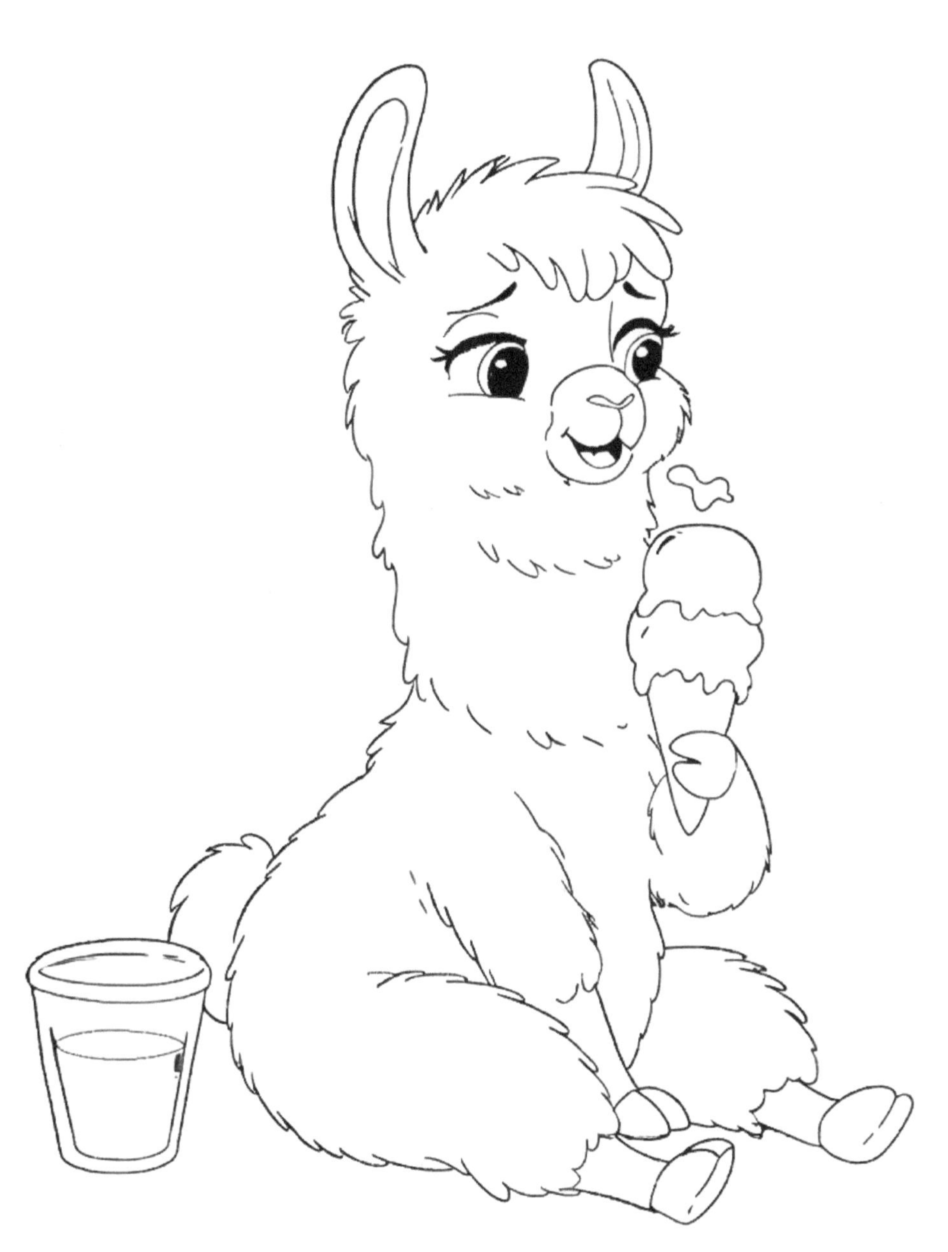

I'm feeling cool in my glasses, ready for you to color me.

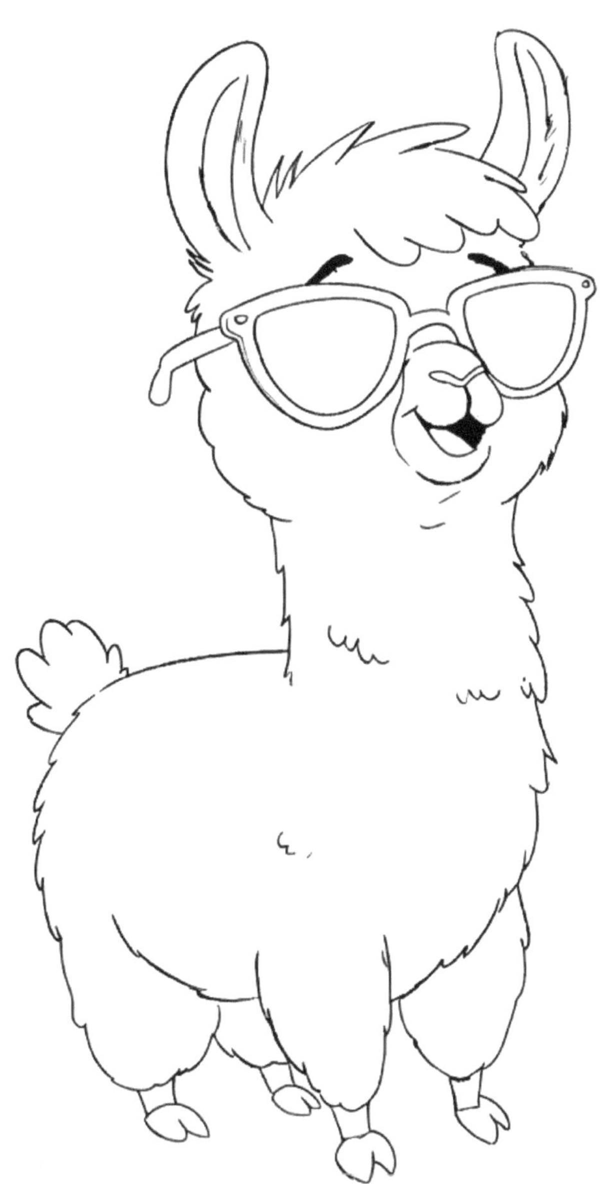

Two little sheep joined me, can you color all three of us?

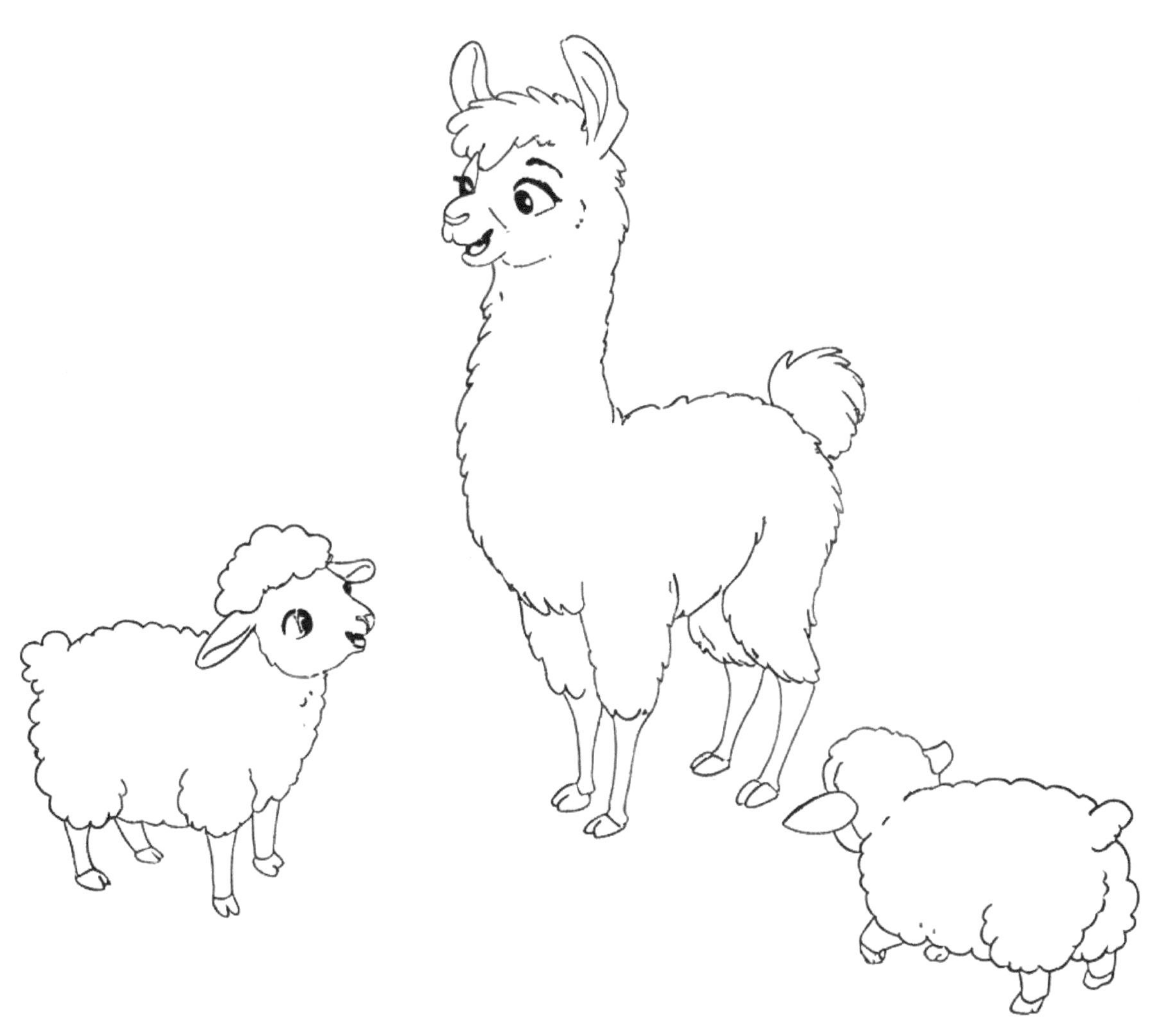

A playful puppy came to visit, color this moment with joy!

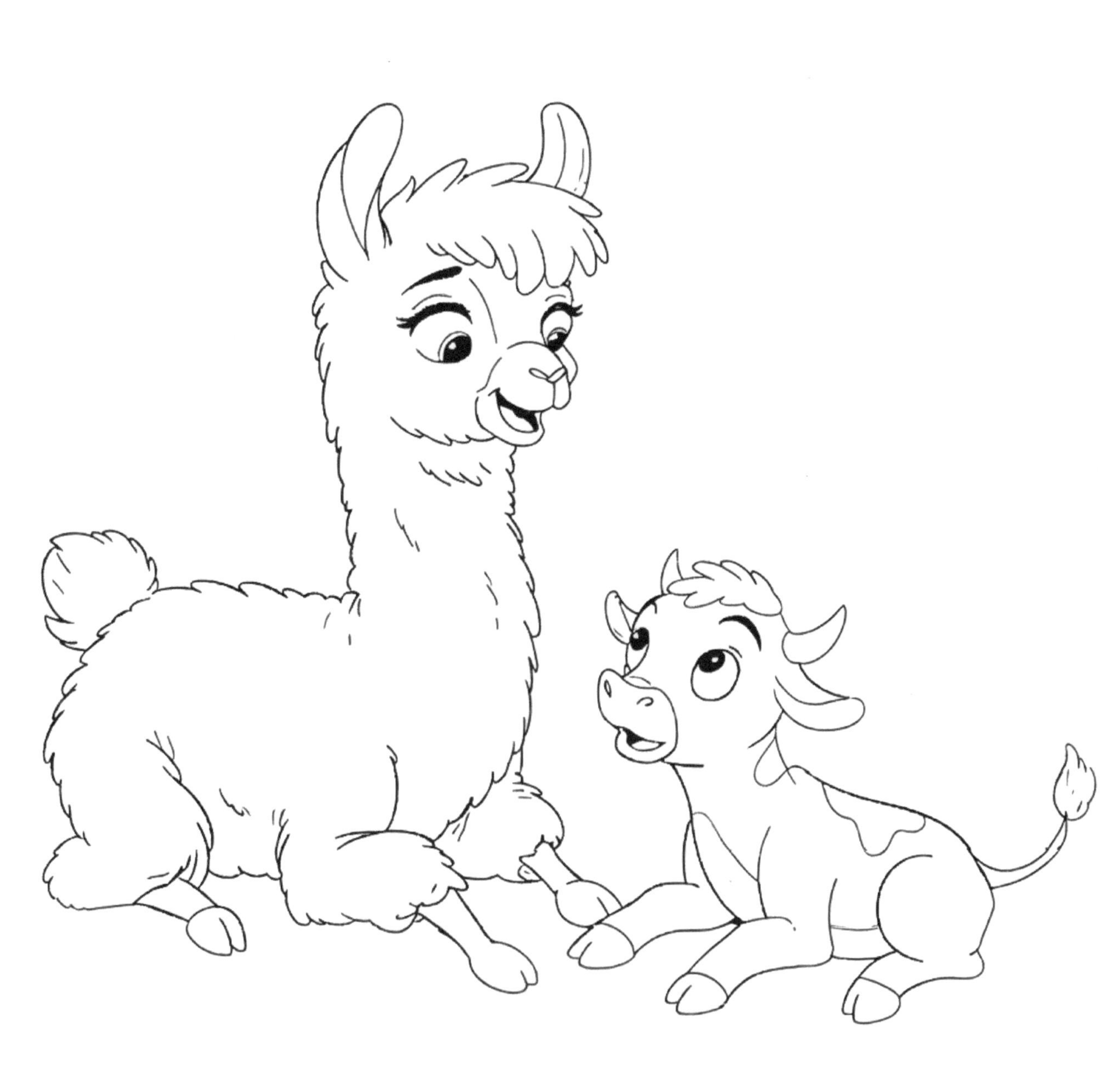

I put on my farm hat today, what color should it be?

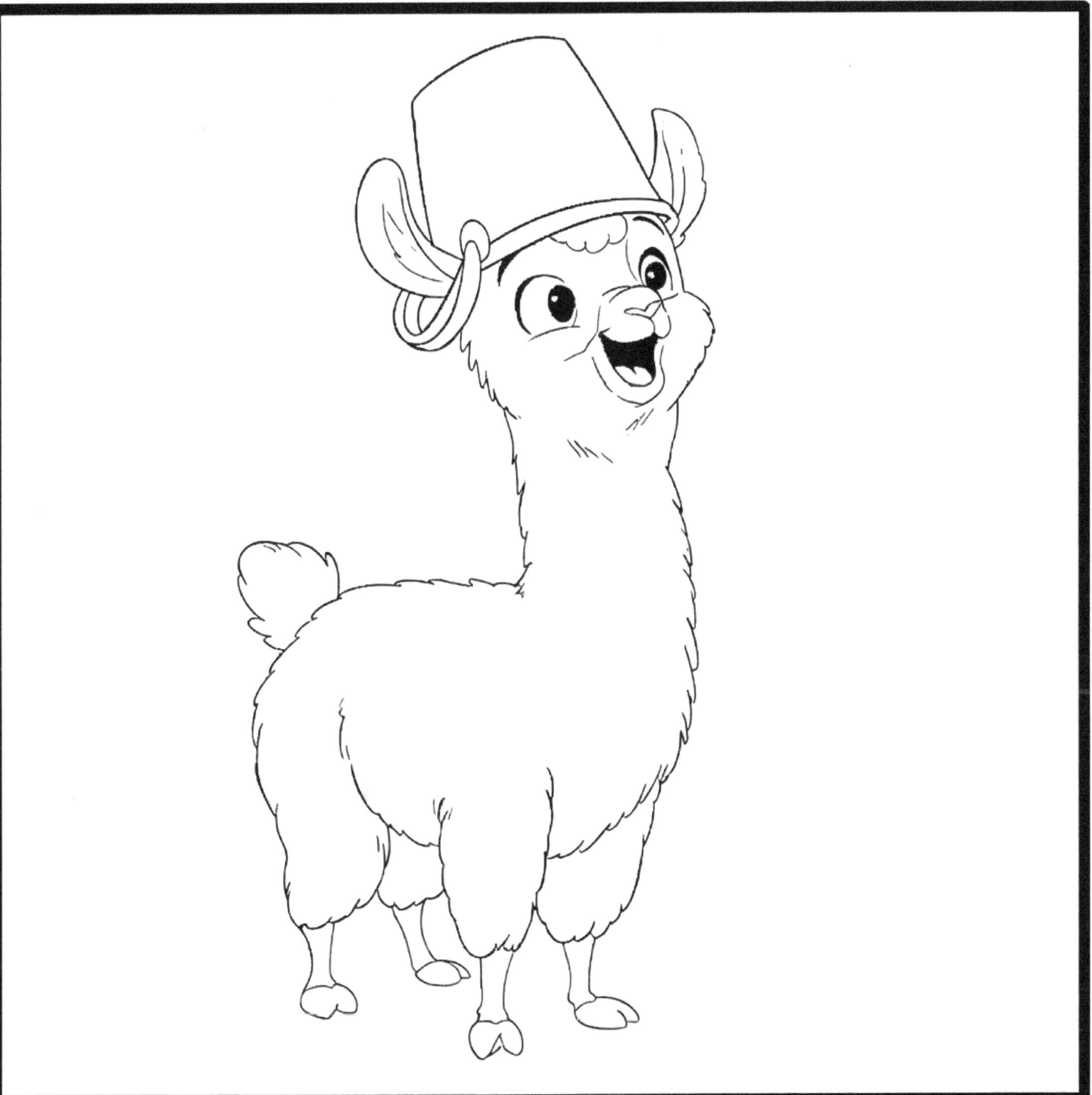

We are a group of llamas
standing together, color
each one differently.

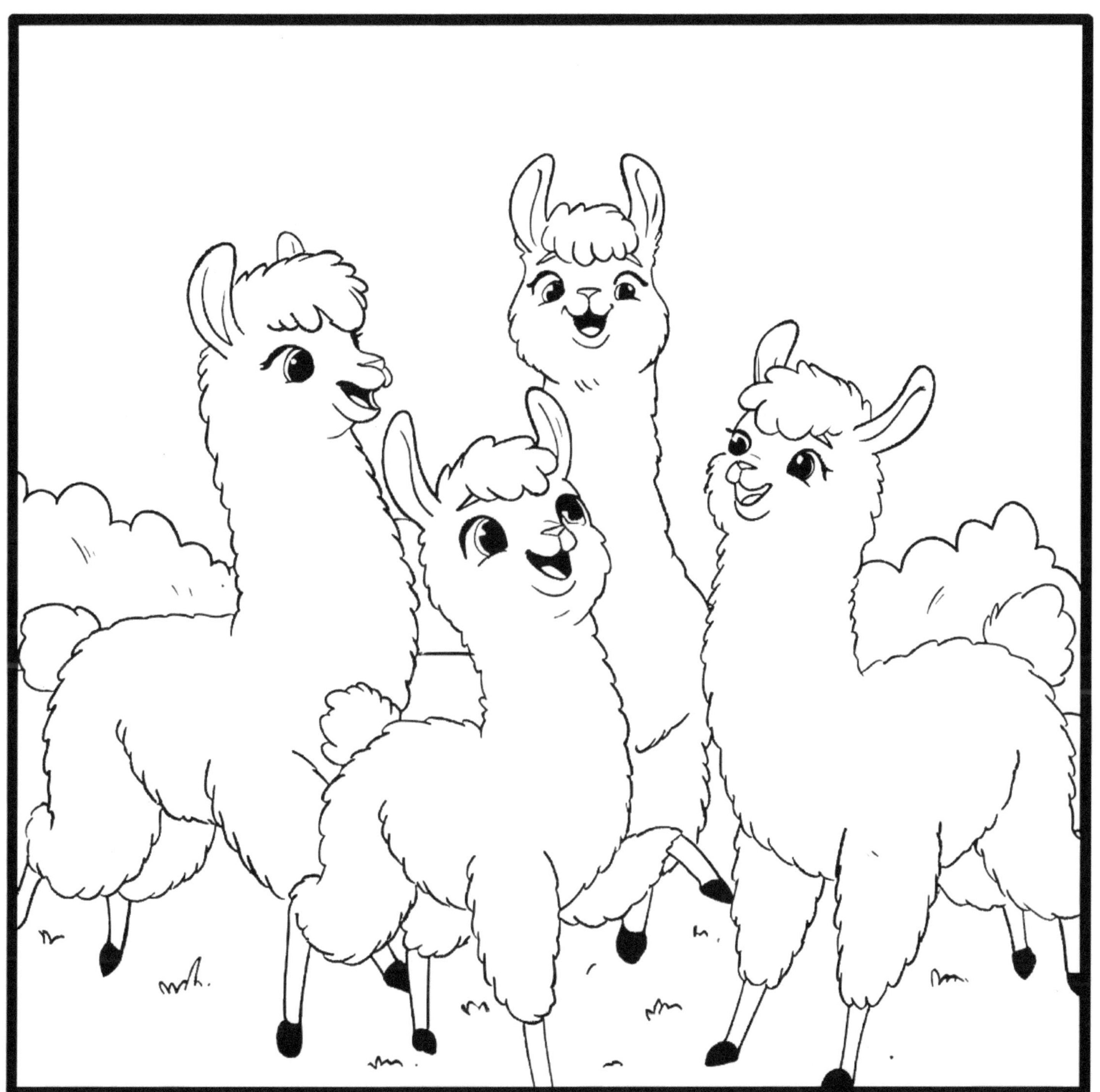